PRAYING IN THE BENEDICTINE SPIRIT

ALAN REES, OSB

MINNEAPOLIS

PRAYING IN THE BENEDICTINE SPIRIT

Copyright © 1999 Alan Rees
Original edition published in English under the
title PRAYING IN THE BENEDICTINE SPIRIT by
Kevin Mayhew Ltd, Buxhall, England.
This edition copyright © Fortress Press 2019

All rights reserved. Except for brief quotations in
critical articles or reviews, no part of this book may be
reproduced in any manner without prior written permission
from the publisher. Email copyright@augsburgfortress.org
or write to Permissions, Fortress Press, PO Box 1209,
Minneapolis, MN 55440-1209.

Cover image: Photo by Halfpoint on iStock
Cover design: Joe Reinke

Print ISBN: 978-1-5064-5959-2

Contents

Introduction	7
THE SEARCH FOR GOD	10
CONVERSION	16
HUMILITY—SURRENDER	21
WORK OF GOD	24
BENEDICTINE SONG	26
REMEMBERING GOD	28
OUR FATHER	32
THE LOVE OF CHRIST MUST COME BEFORE ALL ELSE	33
LISTEN!	39
READING GOD'S WORD	43
THE CROSS	49
BENEDICTINE PEACE	51
FINIS	58
Acknowledgments	59

*Stir up in your church, Lord,
the Spirit in whom our holy father
Benedict served you,
so that filled with the same Spirit,
we may strive to love as he loved
and carry out his teaching.
Through Christ our Lord. Amen.*

Introduction

There was once a man of venerable life whose name was Benedict; and Blessed he was, in grace as well as in name.

Pope St. Gregory the Great begins the second book of his Dialogues with these words. The Dialogues, written probably some fifty years after St. Benedict's death (c 547), are not a full biography by his admirer, but a collection of incidents—some miraculous—in the life of the saint, intended to demonstrate the holiness of Benedict and to instruct the Christians of those days. St. Gregory places great emphasis on the Rule that St. Benedict wrote for monks, and it is this Rule that gives us a lasting impression of the man of God.

Besides the many miracles that made him famous in the world, he was eminent also for his teaching. For he wrote a Rule for Monks which is remarkable both for its discretion and for the lucidity of its style. If anyone wishes to know his character and life more precisely, he may find in the ordinances of that Rule a complete account of the

> *abbot's practice; for the holy man cannot have taught otherwise than as he lived.*
>
> Dialogues, chapter 36[1]

These words of Gregory are still valid at the beginning of the third millennium. If we would understand Benedict's spiritual path, we must go to his Rule. This Rule has inspired monks, nuns, and lay people for over 1500 years. Recent times have seen a flowering of interest in St. Benedict's way and many books have been written to help those living in the world to understand and follow the Rule.

This little book is a simple introduction to the spirituality of St. Benedict. By combining quotations from the Rule and the Psalms, I hope it will highlight the main signposts on St. Benedict's way, and so encourage the readers to take up the Rule themselves and find in it a sure guide in their search for God.

---

1. Trans. Abbot Justin McCann, Stanbrook Abbey Press, 1992

Prayer on the Shrine of St. Benedict at St. Benoit-sur-Loire

Today we are far from home
    and have lost the key to the door
    but you call us to go in
    and find ourselves again.
Your invitation is to the interior life,
    your experience is that of persons
    who regain a sense of themselves.
Benedict teach us the way back to the heart,
    in Christ our Lord. Amen.

. . . the message of Benedict is an invitation to interiority. One should, above all else, enter into oneself, have a profound self-knowledge and find in oneself the footprints of God.

Pope John Paul II[1]

---

[1]. At Monte Cassino, 1979

THE SEARCH FOR GOD

In the Rule of St. Benedict, there is a chapter devoted to the procedure for receiving new members into the community. Benedict says that the monk in charge of novices must make sure that the newcomer "truly seeks God."

This is at the heart of the Benedictine way—the unremitting and sincere search for God in every area of life. Here is the echo of Jesus' invitation in the Gospel to seek first the kingdom of God and his righteousness.

> *Therefore I tell you, do not be anxious about your life, what you shall eat or what you shall drink, nor about your body, what you shall put on. Is not life more than food, and the body more than clothing? But seek first the kingdom of God and his righteousness, and all these things shall be yours as well.*
>
> Matthew 6:25, 33

> *O Lord, hear my voice when I call;*
> *have mercy and answer.*
> *Of you my heart has spoken:*
> *"Seek his face."*

It is your face, O Lord, that I seek;
hide not your face.
Psalm 26:7, 8

You will show me the path of life,
the fullness of joy in your presence,
at your right hand happiness for ever.
Psalm 15:11

I was always in your presence;
you were holding me by my right hand.
You will guide me by your counsel
and so you will lead me to glory.
To be near God is my happiness.
I have made the Lord God my refuge.
Psalm 72:23-4, 28a

God, of your goodness, give me yourself, for you are enough for me.
Julian of Norwich[1]

I am nothing, I have nothing,
I desire nothing, but to see Jesus,
and to be with him in Jerusalem.
Motto of Dom Augustine Baker,
seventeenth-century English Benedictine monk[2]

---

1. *All shall be well*, Sheila Upjohn, Darton, Longman & Todd
2. cf Walter Hilton, *The Scale of Perfection*, Paulist Press, New York, 1991

St. Benedict doesn't care for a life divided into compartments: Sunday for God, Monday for the marketplace. For him the purpose of a monk's life is to give glory to God, not just in church, during prayer, but at every moment. During work, at meal times, while reading, the monk is constantly aware of God's presence, and that his whole life is an act of worship. Benedict makes this clear when he reminds the cellarer—the monk in charge of the practical affairs of the monastery:

> *All the monastery's utensils and goods he should regard as if sacred altar vessels.*
> Rule, chapter 31

> *In all things may God be glorified.*
> Rule, chapter 57

> *I will give you glory, O God my King,*
> *I will bless your name forever.*
> *I will bless you day after day*
> *and praise your name for ever.*
> *The Lord is great, highly to be praised,*
> *his greatness cannot be measured.*
> *Let me speak the praise of the Lord,*

let all mankind bless his holy name,
for ever, for ages unending.
Psalm 144:1-3, 21

There is a tendency at the present time to separate spirituality and ordinary life. People go off in search of something called "spiritual experience" while continuing to lead an unreflecting and materialistic life. Christ has told us that we cannot serve God and mammon. A Christian life has to be a fully integrated life, permeated with God's grace. We have constantly to "seek his face" (Psalm 26) and "seek his kingdom" (Matthew 6). If we truly want to be with God, then we have to turn away from all that is not of God. That is why the idea of conversion is central to Benedictine spirituality.

> *[Moses said to the people] "See, I have set before you this day life and good, death and evil . . . therefore choose life, that you and your descendants may live, loving the Lord your God, obeying his voice, and cleaving to him . . ."*
> Deuteronomy 30:15-20 passim

Lord, make me know your ways.
Lord, teach me your paths.

*Make me walk in your truth and teach me:
for you are God my savior.
The Lord is good and upright.
He shows the path to those who stray.
He guides the humble in the right path;
He teaches his way to the poor.*

Psalm 24:4-5, 8-9

*O search me, God, and know my heart.
O test me and know my thoughts.
See that I follow not the wrong path
and lead me in the path of life eternal.*

Psalm 138:23-24

A Prayer of St. Anselm (1033-1109)
Benedictine Archbishop
of Canterbury

O Lord my God,
  teach my heart where and how to seek you,
  where and how to find you.
Look upon us, Lord, and hear us,
  enlighten us and show yourself to us.

Give yourself to us again that it may be well with us,
>   for without you it is ill with us.
>
> Have mercy on us,
>   as we strive and labour to come to you,
>   for without you we can do nothing well.
>
> Teach me to seek you,
>   and as I seek you, show yourself to me,
>   for I cannot seek you
>   unless you show me how,
>   and I will never find you
>   unless you show yourself to me.
>
> Let me seek you by desiring you,
>   and desire you by seeking you;
>   let me find you by loving you,
>   and love you in finding you.

From The Proslogion [1]

---

[1]. Trans. Sister Benedicta Ward, SLG, Penguin Books

CONVERSION

A Benedictine monk or nun takes a vow of conversion of life. Essentially, this is a Christian's baptismal vow. John the Baptist, the last of the prophets, summed up their message in his call to repentance. The Lord Jesus began his own ministry with these words: "Repent for the kingdom of heaven is at hand." Conversion, repentance—here is the Gospel invitation to those who would be friends of God.

There is no true Christian life unless the heart is turned to the Lord. Benedict tells his disciples that no one can be a good monk unless he gives himself over to the work of conversion.

> *Your way of acting should be different from the world's way;*
> *the love of Christ must come before all else.*

Rule, chapter 4[1]

---

1. *The Rule of St. Benedict in English*, The Liturgical Press, Collegeville, Minnesota 56321, © 1981

I appeal to you . . . by the mercies of God, to present your bodies as a living sacrifice, holy and acceptable to God, which is your spiritual worship. Do not be conformed to this world, but be transformed by the renewing of your minds, so that you may prove what is the will of God—what is good, acceptable and perfect.

Romans 12:1-2

*Remember your mercy, Lord,
and the love you have shown from
of old.
Do not remember the sins of my youth.
In your love remember me.
Lord, for the sake of your name
forgive my guilt; for it is great.*

Psalm 24:6-7, 11

*Indeed you love truth in the heart;
then in the secret of my heart teach
   me wisdom.
O purify me, then I shall be clean;
O wash me, I shall be whiter than snow.
A pure heart create for me, O God,
put a steadfast spirit within me.*

> *Do not cast me away from your presence,
> nor deprive me of your holy spirit.*
>
> Psalm 50:8-9, 12-13

At the same time, Benedict acknowledges that conversion is not an easy thing. In the Prologue to his Rule, we find these words:

> *Do not take fright immediately and run away from the way of salvation. It must be narrow at the start. But as we advance in monastic life and in faith, our hearts will grow, and we shall run with an inexpressible sweetness of love along the way of God's commandments.*
>
> nn 48, 49

> *If anyone fears the Lord
> he will show him the path he should choose.
> His soul shall live in happiness . . .*
>
> Psalm 24:12-13

> *I thank you for your faithfulness and love
> which excel all we ever knew of you.
> On the day I called, you answered;
> you increased the strength of my soul.*
>
> Psalm 137:2-3

In God alone is my soul at rest;
my help comes from him.
He alone is my rock, my stronghold,
my fortress: I stand firm.

Psalm 61:2-3

We have to beware of the quick and easy spiritual "fix" that seems to be so popular today. The road to life is narrow, as Jesus tells us in the Gospel, but it is important to be committed to it because it is the way to God. Those who truly seek him must walk along this narrow road without fear and with perseverance. Jesus, the Way, the Truth, and the Life, has walked that road before us. It is a way that leads through the "valley of the shadow of death" but Christ, our Shepherd and Guide, is with us. Benedict urges us to put our trust in God, in the wisdom of his Word as found in the Scriptures, and then to set out with a sense of purpose and commitment.

And where our nature is powerless, let us ask the Lord to supply the help of his grace . . . If we want to . . . attain everlasting life . . . we must make haste to do at once what will profit us for all eternity.

Prologue to the Rule

*Lord,
may everything we do
begin with your inspiration,
continue with your help,
and reach perfection under your guidance.
Through Christ our Lord. Amen.*
From the Roman Liturgy for Thursday after Ash Wednesday[1] cf. Prologue to the Rule

*Preserve me, O God, I take refuge in you.
I say to the Lord: "You are my God.
My happiness lies in you alone."*
Psalm 15:1-2

*The Lord is my shepherd;
there is nothing I shall want.
If I should walk in the valley of darkness
no evil would I fear.
You are there with your crook and
your staff;
with these you give me comfort.*
Psalm 22:1, 4

---

1. ICEL

HUMILITY—SURRENDER

The first step of humility . . . is for someone to keep the fear of God before his eyes at all times and never forget it.
Rule, chapter 7

True humility depends on our being continually aware of God's presence, and that we exist, not for our own ends, but for the praise of his glory. God is our Creator and we are his creatures; we depend on him for everything. He is our Father, who wants to give us everything, so we approach him with reverence, with love and with open hands. This is the *fear of the Lord*—not a servile attitude but the open and trusting hearts of devoted sons and daughters. In this we have the example of the Lord Jesus and his Mother, Mary.

Have this mind among yourselves, which is yours in Christ Jesus, who, though he was in the form of God, did not count equality with God a thing to be grasped, but emptied himself, taking the form of a servant, being born in the likeness of men. And being found in human form he humbled himself and became obedient unto death, even death on a cross.

Philippians 2:5-8

*My soul magnifies the Lord
and my spirit rejoices in God my Savior,
for he has regarded the low estate of his
   handmaiden . . .
He has shown strength with his arm,
he has scattered the proud in the imagination
   of their hearts,
he has put down the mighty from their thrones,
and exalted those of low degree.*

Mary's song, Luke 1:46-8, 51-2

*To put one's hope in God.
To attribute to God and not to self, whatever good one may see in one's self.*

Rule, chapter 4

A monk makes a complete surrender of himself to God when he makes his vows for life. After prostrating himself on the ground, he stands before the altar and sings:

*If you uphold me by your promise I shall live;
let my hopes not be in vain.*

Psalm 118:116

This attitude of deep trust in God's promises and purposes permeates the life of the monk. To live, work, and pray in the knowledge that, in the Lord Jesus, one is truly beloved of the Father gives great strength and joy in all the changing scenes of life.

In prayer, we come before God humbly, in trust and complete surrender, and remembering our weak and sinful state, we make our own the prayer of the publican in the Gospel:

God, be merciful to me, a sinner.

Luke 18:13

Whenever we want to ask something from powerful people, we do not presume to do so without humility and respect. How much more ought we to pray to the Lord God of all things with profound humility and pure devotion. And we must realise that we shall be heard not for our many words, but for our purity of heart and tears of compunction.

Rule, chapter 20

WORK OF GOD

As darkness gives way to dawn, and hour to hour in the rhythm of God's created order, so monks and nuns gather together several times each day to sanctify the passage of time with prayer and praise. St. Benedict bids us be aware of God's presence at all times but the continuing dialogue with God is sustained and nourished by these strong points of common prayer. This is called the Divine Office or Work of God—*Opus Dei*, to use St. Benedict's term. Prayer, in the first place, is God's work in us, but we too have to work at prayer by regularity and attention.

> *We believe that God's presence is everywhere, and that "in every place the eyes of the Lord are watching the good and the bad". Especially ought we to believe this, without the slightest doubt, when we are celebrating the divine office.*

Rule, chapter 19

*I rise before dawn and cry for help,
I hope in your word.*

*My eyes watch through the night
to ponder your promise.
Seven times a day I praise you
for your just decrees.*
Psalm 118:147-8, 164

BENEDICTINE SONG

*In the presence of the angels
I will sing to you, O Lord*

Psalm 137:1[1]

Singing has always been associated with monastic prayer. Benedictines celebrate the Divine Office and Mass with solemnity and song. Until the liturgical renewal which came with the Second Vatican Council, the liturgy was celebrated in Latin and sung to Gregorian chant. The renewal of interest in Gregorian chant, the ancient melodies of the Church's worship, was sparked by the reissue of recordings made by the Benedictine monks of Silos in Spain some years ago. Gregorian chant still has pride of place, but new melodies, often inspired by the modality of the old chants, have been written for the vernacular liturgy. For monks and nuns, singing is an integral part of their worship. Monastic chant is sung prayer—as St. Augustine tells us, "He who sings, prays twice." Lay people who attend the liturgy in monastic houses are often inspired by the singing of the psalms in the office, and can join in with the monks and nuns. Many communities have made recordings, in Latin and English,

---

1. From the Latin of the Rule

and these can be an aid to personal prayer and meditation at home.

> *Sing praise for God, sing praise,*
> *sing praise to our king, sing praise.*
> *God is king of all the earth.*
> *Sing praise with all your skill.*
>
> Psalm 46:7-8

> *O sing a new song to the Lord,*
> *sing to the Lord all the earth.*
> *O sing to the Lord, bless his name.*
> *Bring an offering and enter his courts,*
> *worship the Lord in his temple.*
>
> Psalm 95:1-2, 8-9

> *I will sing to the Lord all my life,*
> *make music to my God while I live.*
> *May my thoughts be pleasing to him.*
> *I find my joy in the Lord.*
>
> Psalm 103:33-34

REMEMBERING GOD

In the Old Testament, the Israelites were frequently berated by the prophets for forgetting God and all the wonders he had done for them. We too can be forgetful of God and over-absorbed in ourselves and our occupations.

In the life of the Church, and so in the monastic life, the memory of God is kept alive continually in the Eucharist and the Divine Office.

> *This is my Body, given for you . . .*
> *This is my Blood poured out for you . . .*
> *do this in memory of me.*

The daily recitation of the Book of Psalms (the Psalter)—the Church's Prayer Book—makes up the greater part of the Divine Office. Here we call to mind God's mercies in the past and present, and seek his providential care in the future. The psalms are filled with praise and thanksgiving for God's wonderful works, and seek out his help in grief and suffering, his mercy in sinfulness. The hours of the Divine Office continually make us mindful of God's presence in our lives through the inspired words of the psalms and other books of the Bible.

A newcomer to the Benedictine life must have an "eagerness for the Work of God" (Rule, chapter 58). This eagerness continues throughout the lives of the monks because "as soon as the signal for an hour of the Divine Office is heard, they should lay aside whatever they have in hand and assemble as quickly as possible, yet in a dignified manner . . . nothing, indeed, should be put before the Work of God" (Rule, chapter 43).

This speaks to us of the priority of God in our lives, and the necessity of talking to him frequently. Most people who take their Christian lives seriously give time to prayer, especially at the beginning and end of the day. But it is also important to be aware of God's presence throughout the day, and to pause briefly in the midst of our occupations and leisure to raise our hearts and minds to him.

> *Prayer, therefore, ought always to be short and pure, unless perhaps prolonged by the inspiration of God's grace*
> Rule, chapter 20

Some people like to say the hours of the Divine Office, but not all have the time for this. Everyone, however, can call to mind God's presence in a brief moment of silent prayer at intervals during the day. It is a good practice to commit to memory brief lines from the psalms that will then come readily to our lips when our prayer is dry or distracted. All can capture the spirit of the Divine Office by memorizing phrases from the various hours, such as the opening of Matins:

> *O Lord, open my lips*
> *and my mouth shall declare your praise.*
> Psalm 50:17

The ancient Fathers of the Desert recommended that, during the course of the day, we use frequently the text with which we begin the other hours:

> *O God, come to my aid.*
> *O Lord, make haste to help me!*
> Psalm 69:2

Other short prayers from the office will also help us to recollect our thoughts and focus them on God during the day:

> *Lord, have mercy. Christ, have mercy.*
> *Lord, have mercy.*

> *To you our praise is due; we hymn your glory, Father, Son and Holy Spirit.*
>
> *May God's assistance be with us always, and with our absent brothers and sisters. Amen.*

Other verses of the psalms suggested in this book may be helpful on different occasions. Many people use the Jesus Prayer, which comes from the Eastern tradition of Christianity:

> *Lord Jesus Christ, Son of God, have mercy on me a sinner.*

At the end of the day, the antiphon of the Song of Simeon and the blessing from Compline make a fitting conclusion to our prayer:

> *Save us, Lord, while waking and guard us while sleeping, that awake we may watch with Christ and asleep we may rest in peace.*
>
> *May the Lord grant us a quiet night and a perfect end. Amen.*

OUR FATHER

Of course, the offices of Lauds and Vespers ought never to end without the superior finally reciting, for all to hear, the whole of the Lord's Prayer, on account of the thorns of contention that frequently spring up. Warned as they are by the covenant made in the words of that prayer, "forgive us as we forgive", may they themselves be cleansed of such faults. Rule, chapter 13

The prayer Jesus taught us is the pattern of all prayer. In whatever circumstances we may say the Lord's Prayer, we will find that one of the seven petitions will have a particular significance for us. For Benedict it has to be recited with a certain solemnity at the end of morning and evening prayer, especially that we may be reminded of the importance of forgiveness. At the cross, Jesus prayed, "Forgive them, Father, they do not know what they are doing." These words must resonate in our own lives and be expressed in our daily prayer if we would grow in love for one another. God's kingdom can come and his will can be done only in hearts and minds that are open in love, compassion, and truth to his creation and to his creatures. Let us be sure to say the words of the Lord's Prayer with reverence and care, making our own each word given us by the Savior.

THE LOVE OF CHRIST MUST COME BEFORE ALL ELSE
Rule, chapter 4

St. Benedict calls his monastery "a school of the Lord's service" where the commandments of God are learned and lived. In the first place, of course, is the commandment to love God and one another as Christ has loved us. From the abbot to the youngest member of the community, there has to be mutual love and regard.

> *This, then, is the good zeal which monks must foster with fervent love: they should each try to be the first to show respect to the other (Romans 12:10), supporting with the greatest patience one another's weaknesses of body and behaviour . . . No one is to pursue what he judges better for himself, but instead, what he judges better for someone else . . . To their fellow monks they show the pure love of brothers; to God, loving fear; to their abbot, unfeigned and humble love. Let them prefer nothing whatever to Christ, and may he bring us all together to everlasting life.*
>
> Rule, chapter 72[1]

---

1. *The Rule of St. Benedict in English*, The Liturgical Press, Collegeville, Minnesota 56321, © 1981

But especially is this love to be shown to guests, the poor, and to pilgrims. The hospitality offered in the monastery is not grudging but generous and open-hearted, because through it Christ is loved and served in a special way.

> *All guests who present themselves are to be welcomed as Christ, for he himself will say: "I was a stranger and you welcomed me" (Matthew 25:35). Once a guest has been announced, the superior and the brothers are to meet him with all the courtesy of love.*
> *First of all, they are to pray together and thus be united in peace . . .*
>
> *By a bow of the head or by a complete prostration of the body, Christ is to be adored because he is indeed welcomed in them.*
>
> *Great care and concern are to be shown in receiving poor people and pilgrims, because in them more particularly Christ is received.*
>
> Rule chapter 53[1]

---

1. *The Rule of St. Benedict in English*, The Liturgical Press, Collegeville, Minnesota 56321, © 1981

In the passages on the reception of guests, St. Benedict shows that we are worshiping Christ by our attitude of humility, love, and service to all who we meet. He makes no distinction between brothers and strangers—Christ is received and adored in all.

> *Whatever you do to the least of my brethren, you do it to me.*
> Matthew 25:40

St. Paul has the same message in his letters to the Romans and Corinthians:

> *Let love be genuine; hate what is evil, hold fast to what is good; love one another with brotherly affection; outdo one another in showing honor.*
> Romans 12:9-10

> *. . . if I am lacking in love, I am nothing.*
> 1 Corinthians 13:2

Every day, we have many opportunities for receiving and adoring Christ in our brothers and sisters. St. Benedict sets before us a way of life based on love—it is the way Christ offers us—and we have so many opportunities for walking along this way of love. Do we see Jesus in those we meet every day: members of our family, our friends, the sorrowful, the poor, the sick, those marginalized by society, not to mention those we find unpleasant and difficult, our "enemies"? Do we meet them with generosity, forgiveness, openness, and love? The words we utter in our prayers are put into action when we open our hearts in love for our neighbor.

> *But I say to you: Love your enemies and pray for those who persecute you, so that you may be children of your Father who is in heaven; for he makes his sun rise on the evil and on the good, and sends rain on the just and the unjust. For if you love those who love you, what reward do you have?*
> Matthew 5:44-46

> *Lord, our help and guide,*
> *make your love the foundation of our lives.*
> *May our love for you express itself*

in our eagerness to do good for others.
Through Christ our Lord. Amen.
Roman Missal, Twenty-eighth Sunday of the Year[1]

Where charity and love are found, there is God.

The love of Christ has gathered us together into one.
Let us rejoice and be glad in him.
Let us fear and love the living God,
and let us love each other from the depths of our heart.

Where charity and love are found, there is God.

Therefore when we are together,
let us take heed not to be divided in mind.
Let there be an end to bitterness and quarrels, an end to strife,
and in our midst be Christ our God.

Where charity and love are found, there is God.

And in company with the blessed, may we see

---

1. ICEL

*your face in glory, Christ our God,
pure and unbounded joy
for ever and ever.*

Roman Missal: Mass of the Lord's Supper[1]

---

1. ICEL

LISTEN!

The Rule of St. Benedict begins

> *Listen carefully, my child, to the teaching of the master and bend close the ear of your heart.*

In a world so full of noise and action, it is not easy to slow down and be quiet. Yet, if we would hear God's voice, we must cultivate an attitude of listening; we must enter the silence of the universe and listen for that "still, small voice of calm"

> *I will hear what the Lord God has to say, a voice that speaks of peace.*
> Psalm 84:9

> *Be still and know that I am God.*
> Psalm 45:11

You will notice that Benedict bids us "bend close the ear of your heart." God speaks to us in all sorts of ways—in the beauty of creation, in the events of the world and of our own lives, but he especially speaks in his Word that comes to us in the Holy Scriptures, the Bible. We must allow God's word to speak to our heart, to resonate in the whole of our being. We must be still and listen. St. Paul tells the early Christians to "let the Word of Christ, in all its richness, find a home with you" (Colossians 3:16[1]).

Prayer of St. Bede the Venerable

> I pray you Good Jesus
> > that as you have given me the grace
> > to drink in with joy
> > the Word that gives knowledge of you,
> > so in your goodness
> > you will grant me to come at length
> > to Yourself, the Source of all Wisdom,
> > to stand before your face forever.

St. Benedict enjoins on the members of his communities a certain amount of silence. This is necessary in order to cultivate an inner stillness which helps quiet all those alien voices that can drown out the voice of God in our lives. All who would follow the way of St. Benedict will take heed of his advice by resisting the temptation to be overactive, by resisting the temptation to be always listening to the radio, or watching the television. Create a little space in your life and fill it with silence, a silence where we can listen for the voice of God—in the beauty of the created order,

---

[1]. New Jerusalem Bible

in the voice of suffering humanity, in the quiet of prayer, in the words of Scripture.

> *I have taken no part in great affairs,*
> *in wonders beyond my scope.*
> *No, I hold myself in quiet and silence,*
> *like a little child in its mother's arms,*
> *like a little child, so I keep myself.*
> Psalm 130[1]

In medieval times, the monks rose in the middle of the night, in darkness and silence, and gathered in a dimly lit church to hear God's Word as they kept vigil. Given the pace of modern life, an "all-night vigil" is a rare event for us. But we can make the effort to create some opportunity for silence in our lives, and to distance ourselves from all that distracts us—both externally and internally. We are creating a place to meet God, where he can find a home with us. By turning from sin, and from all that is not of God, we are preparing a home for him where he will come and be our companion.

> *Look, I am standing at the door, knocking. If one of you hears me calling and opens the door, I will come in to share a meal at that person's side.*
> Revelation 3:20[1]

---

1. New Jerusalem Bible

Seek me out, Lord, call to me, bid me come out of my hiding place and welcome you into my home.

Sit at my table, eat with me, listen to my story, have pity on me and forgive my preoccupation with the trivialities of life which prevent me from coming to you. Bring salvation to my house and my heart will rejoice.[1]

---

1. From *Prayers from the Cloister*, Alan Rees, OSB. Kevin Mayhew, 1996

READING GOD'S WORD

Idleness is the enemy of the soul. Therefore, at given times the brethren ought to be occupied in manual labour, and again at other times in prayerful reading.

Rule, chapter 48[1]

Indeed, what page or what passage of the divinely inspired books of the Old and New Testaments is not an infallible guide for human life?

Rule, chapter 73[1]

The monastic day is given over to the prayer of the Divine Office, holy reading, and work, and the monk seeks God and dwells in his presence in each of these areas of his life. For St. Benedict, the time given to holy reading (Lectio Divina) is a very special moment of union with God, for it is in the Scriptures that God speaks to us through the words of the law and prophets, the wisdom literature, the psalms, and particularly through the message of life spoken by Jesus, the Word made flesh.

To listen eagerly to holy reading. To devote oneself frequently to prayer.

Rule, chapter 4[1]

1. *The Rule of St. Benedict in English*, The Liturgical Press, Collegeville, Minnesota 56321, © 1981

This time of prayerful reading is not just "Bible study"—it is a dialogue between the reader and God. We read his word with open, attentive hearts, and absorb it into our very depths; allowing it to work within us, we then respond prayerfully to what God is saying to us in that particular passage of Scripture.

> *The word of God is living and active, sharper than any two-edged sword, piercing to the division of soul and spirit, of joints and marrow, and discerning the thoughts and intentions of the heart.*
> Hebrews 4:12

> *I have come that you may have life and have it in abundance.*
> *Your words are spirit, Lord, and they are life.*
> John 10:10 and cf. John 6:63

> *Your word is a lamp for my steps and a light for my path.*
> Psalm 118:105

My soul lies in the dust;
by your word revive me.
Psalm 118:25

Let us pray for the grace to respond to the Word of God:
God our Father, help us to hear your Son.
Enlighten us with your word,
that we may find the way to your glory.
Collect for Second Sunday of Lent[1]

Blessed Lord, who caused all holy Scriptures to be written for our learning: help us so to hear them, to read, mark, learn and inwardly digest them that, through patience, and the comfort of your holy word, we may embrace and ever hold fast the hope of everlasting life, which you have given us in our Savior, Jesus Christ.
Collect for Second Sunday of Advent[2]

In the sacred books the Father who is in heaven comes lovingly to meet his children and talks with them . . . and such is the force and power of

---

1. Roman Missal, ICEL 2. The Alternative Service Book, 1980

the Word of God that it can serve the Church as her support and vigour, and the children of the Church as strength for their faith, food for their soul, and a pure and lasting fount of spiritual life.[1]

This is lectio, the monastic way of praying with a phrase from Scripture, repeating it, rocking it back and forwards, letting it move into the depths of one's own self until it goes beyond words into silence, into contemplation.[2]

Seek in reading and you will find in meditating, knock in prayer and it will be opened to you in contemplation.
Guigo the Carthusian

LECTIO DIVINA — A METHOD OF PRAYING THE SCRIPTURES

1. **A quiet place and a quiet mind**
   Create a place of silence within you and around you, and direct your attention to this meeting with God in Holy Scripture.

---

1. Documents of Vatican II, "Dei Verbum" #21, Flannery
2. *The Celtic Way of Prayer*, Esther de Waal, Hodder & Stoughton

2. "Then he opened their minds to understand the Scriptures" (Luke 24:45).
   We ask the Lord Jesus to give us the Spirit of wisdom and understanding, and to take away from us all that makes us unreceptive to his word, especially the sin that can darken our minds.

3. Mary became the dwelling place of the Divine Word.
   We ask her to accompany us in this time of prayerful reading.

4. Read a little, slowly, forming the words with your lips (aloud or quietly).
   Keep the heart alert, let the words find their way to your heart, keep your mind attentive.

5. When something strikes you—stop!
   Repeat that phrase or sentence—several times: let it sink into your heart.

6. Your response—how does this word affect me? What is it saying to me, what is it saying about the way I live?
   Is it a word of correction or encouragement?

Does it enkindle within me sorrow for sin, thanksgiving, praise, intercession?

7. Stay with this word until you have received all the nourishment possible at that moment.

8. Continue, if time allows—have a fixed time.

9. End by making some resolution, by praying for someone.
   Let your prayer be formed by what you have read.

10. If it helps, write down anything that strikes you during Lectio.
    Your notes will be a useful aid to prayer in the future.

> *Almighty God, we thank you for the gift of*
>   *your holy Word.*
> *May it be a lantern to our feet, a light to*
> *our paths, and a strength to our lives.*
> *Take us and use us to love and serve*
>   *all people*
> *in the power of the Holy Spirit*
> *and in the name of your Son,*
> *Jesus Christ our Lord. Amen.*[1]

---

1. Alternative Service Book, 1980

THE CROSS

St. Gregory, in the *Dialogues*, tells the story of St. Benedict being asked by some monks to be their abbot. However, because of their evil intent, these monks did not want to follow the way of life set before them by the holy man. They gave him a cup of poison to drink with his meal, but when Benedict blessed the table with the sign of the cross before the meal, the cup shattered and revealed the sin of the monks. St. Benedict is often depicted holding the cross and the poisoned chalice—a reminder that Jesus, by his cross and resurrection, has set us free from evil. In our prayer, we make the sign of the cross with great reverence and thanksgiving for the victory of Jesus, and we ask that we may experience the power of his victory in all our temptation and suffering.

> *We worship you, Lord,*
> *we venerate your cross,*
> *we praise your resurrection.*
> *Through the cross you brought joy to*
> *the world.*
> Antiphon from the Liturgy of Good Friday[1]
>
> *May the holy cross be my light.*
> Medal of St. Benedict

1. ICEL

May I come to know Christ and the power of his resurrection,
and partake of his sufferings by being moulded to the pattern of his death, striving towards the goal of resurrection from the dead.

After St. Paul, Philippians 3:10-11[1]

---

1. New Jerusalem Bible

BENEDICTINE PEACE

The age-old motto of the Benedictines is Pax—peace.

In making provision for the ordering of his household, St. Benedict is always aware of the need for peace that comes from good order in daily life. Quoting Psalm 33 in the Prologue, he says, "If you desire true and eternal life . . . *let peace be your quest and aim.*" In chapter 4 he reminds the brethren that they must never give a hollow greeting of peace and they must always make peace with each other before sundown. In a later chapter (34), he explains how all should have what they need and there must be no word or sign of the evil of grumbling—*"in this way all the members will be at peace."* All the decisions in the conduct of the monastery must be made by the abbot *"for the preservation of peace and love"* (chapter 65). St. Benedict is showing us the value and necessity of peace within a group of people who are truly seeking God; indeed, it is the hallmark of such a community. Here he is merely echoing the words of the psalms, and of Jesus and his apostles.

*How good and how pleasant it is,
when brothers live together in unity!*
Psalm 132:1

*Truly I have set my soul
in silence and peace.*
Psalm 130:2

*I will hear what the Lord God has to say,
a voice that speaks of peace,
peace for his people and his friends
and those who turn to him in their hearts.
His help is near for those who fear him
and his glory will dwell in our land.*
Psalm 84:9-10

*For the peace of Jerusalem pray:
"Peace be to your homes!
May peace reign in your walls,
in your palaces, peace!"
For love of my brethren and friends
I say: "Peace upon you!"
For love of the house of the Lord
I will ask for your good.*
Psalm 121:6-9

All who desire God yearn for the peace of the new Jerusalem, where we shall see God face to face. Our desire for peace is quickened as we contemplate the century of wars that we have just passed through; we yearn for that peace which Jesus promised—"*a peace the world cannot give."* We can identify with the writer of Psalm 119:

> *Long enough have I been dwelling*
> *with those who hate peace.*
> *I am for peace, but when I speak,*
> *they are for fighting.*
> Psalm 119:6-7

The Hebrew greeting *Shalom* means so much more than our English word "peace." The Israelite believed that peace is a gift of God, and so within the greeting was contained the wish for all the goodness of God to be bestowed upon the receiver; not only absence of war and strife, but a perfect communion with the Lord. The Messiah is the Prince of Peace and in his kingdom there is peace without end. St. Benedict is striving to make his monastic communities places where the peace of God's kingdom is truly experienced. So, this peace is not something we seek only for the future, it is the blessing we ask in the midst of the chaos of daily life. Charity begins at home, so does peace. Like St. Benedict, we have to work at peace in the context of our daily family life. We shall take care to be fair and just in our decisions, to be kind and forgiving in our relationships so that peace will reign in the hearts of all.

And we need peace within ourselves. So often we feel at odds within—shadows of guilt and shame, the bitter taste of resentment or unforgiveness, brittle feelings of envy or jealousy. God calls us to turn away from sin and from all those things that disturb our inner peace, and to accept his love, mercy, and forgiveness, from which flows the "peace that surpasses all understanding."

> *Peace I leave with you; my peace I give to you; not as the world gives do I give to you. Let not your hearts be troubled, neither let them be afraid.*
> John 14:27

> *Deliver us, Lord, from every evil,*
> *and grant us peace in our day.*
> *In your mercy keep us free from sin*
> *and protect us from all anxiety*
> *as we wait in joyful hope*

for the coming of our Savior, Jesus Christ.
For the kingdom, the power, and the glory are yours,
now and for ever.
Roman Missal: Order of Mass[1]

Lord Jesus Christ, you said to your apostles:
I leave you peace, my peace I give you.
Look not on our sins,
but on the faith of your Church,
And grant us the peace and unity of your kingdom
Where you live for ever and ever.
Amen.[1]

Lamb of God, you take away the sins of the world: grant us peace.
Roman Missal: Order of Mass[1]

Put on then, as God's chosen ones, holy and beloved, compassion, kindness, lowliness, meekness and patience, forbearing one another and, if one has a complaint against another, forgiving each other; as the Lord has forgiven you, so you also must forgive. And

1. ICEL

> *above all these put on love, which binds everything together in perfect harmony. And let the peace of Christ rule in your hearts, to which indeed you were called in one body.*
>
> Colossians 3:12-15

In a world so beset by war, violence, racial intolerance, and fear, we need "to seek peace and pursue it"—we need to pray daily for peace, and to cooperate with people of goodwill and sincere heart in the search for all those things that are good and true and make for peace.

> *Father in heaven,*
> *form in us the likeness of your Son*
> *and deepen his life within us.*
> *Send us as witnesses of gospel joy*
> *into a world of fragile peace and broken*
>   *promises.*
> *Touch the hearts of all with your love*
> *that they in turn may love one another.*
> *We ask this through Christ our Lord.*
>
> Roman Missal: Eighth Sunday of the Year[1]

> *Almighty Father,*
> *the love you offer*
> *always exceeds the furthest expression of*

---

1. ICEL

our human longing,
for you are greater than the human heart.

Direct each thought, each effort of our life,
so that the limits of our faults
  and weaknesses
may not obscure the vision of your glory
or keep us from the peace you
  have promised.
We ask this through Christ our Lord.
Roman Missal: Third Sunday of the Year[1]

---

1. ICEL

FINIS

As we advance in monastic life and in faith, our hearts will grow, and we shall run with an inexpressible sweetness of love along the way of God's commandments; so that never deviating from his precepts but persevering in his teaching in the monastery until death, we shall share by patience in the sufferings of Christ, that we may deserve to share also in his kingdom. Amen.

End of the Prologue to the Rule

The end of all things is near; therefore be serious and discipline yourselves for the sake of your prayers. Above all, maintain constant love for one another, for love covers a multitude of sins. Be hospitable to one another without complaining. Like good stewards of the manifold grace of God, serve one another with whatever gift each of you has received. Whoever speaks must do so as one speaking the very words of God; whoever serves must do so with the strength that God supplies, so that God may be glorified in all things through Jesus Christ. To him belong the glory and power for ever and ever. Amen.

1 Peter 4:7-11[1]

---

1. New Revised Standard Version

Acknowledgments

I should like to thank Abbot Francis Rossiter, Abbot Mark Jabalé, Dame Anne Field, and members of the Belmont Community for their helpful comments and suggestions.

Scriptures are taken from the *Revised Standard Version* of the Bible unless otherwise indicated.

Psalms are quoted from *The Grail*.

Quotations from the Rule of St. Benedict taken from *Work and Prayer*, trans. Catherine Wybourne, OSB, Burns and Oates 1992, unless otherwise indicated.

The publishers wish to express their gratitude to the following for permission to include copyright material in this book:

The Archbishops' Council, Church House, Great Smith Street, London, SW1P 3NZ, for the extracts from the *Alternative Service Book 1980*, © The Archbishops' Council of the Church of England, 1980; The Archbishops' Council 1999.

Burns & Oates (an imprint of Search Press Ltd), Wellwood, North Farm Road, Tunbridge Wells, Kent, TN2 3DR, for the extracts from *The Rule of St. Benedict for laypeople*, translated by Abbot Justin McCann.

Darton, Longman & Todd Ltd, 1 Spencer Court, 140-142 Wandsworth High Street, London, SW18 4JJ, for the Bible quotations which are taken from the *New Jerusalem Bible*, © 1985 Darton, Longman & Todd Ltd and Doubleday & Co. Inc.

The International Commission on English in the Liturgy (ICEL), 1522 K Street, NW, Suite 1000, Washington DC, 20005-1202, USA, for excerpts from the English translation of *The Roman Missal*, © 1973 International Committee on English in the Liturgy, Inc. All rights reserved.

The Liturgical Press, St. John's Abbey, PO Box 7500, Collegeville, MN 56321-7500, for the extracts from *The Rule of St. Benedict in English*, © 1981 The Order of St. Benedict, Inc.

Penguin UK, 27 Wrights Lane, Kensington, London, W8 5TZ, for the Prayer of St. Anselm, taken from *The Proslogion*, translated by Sister Benedicta Ward, SLG.

Stanbrook Abbey Press, Callow End, Worcester, WR2 4TD, for the extracts from *Dialogues of St. Gregory*, translated by Justin McCann, © 1992 Stanbrook Abbey.

A. P. Watt Ltd, 20 John Street, London, WC1N 2DR (on behalf of The Grail), for the Psalms which are taken from *The Grail Translation: New Inclusive Language Version*.

Every effort has been made to trace copyright owners of material and we hope that no copyright has been infringed. Pardon is sought and apology made if the contrary be the case, and a correction will be made in any reprint of this book.

www.ingramcontent.com/pod-product-compliance
Lightning Source LLC
Chambersburg PA
CBHW071222070526
44584CB00019B/3127